SELECTED

Other Works by Ronald Duncan

POETRY

Postcards to Pulcinella
The Mongrel
The Solitudes
Man (Parts I-V)
Judas
Unpopular Poems
For the Few

PLAYS

The Dull Ass's Hoof
This Way to the Tomb
Stratton
The Rape of Lucretia
Don Juan
Our Lady's Tumbler
The Death of Satan
Abelard and Héloïse
The Catalyst
O.B.A.F.G.
Selected Plays

PROSE

Journal of a Husbandman
Home-Made Home
Tobacco Growing in England
The Blue Fox
Jan's Journal
The Last Adam
Saint Spiv
The Perfect Mistress
The Kettle of Fish
The Tale of Tails
The Encyclopaedia of Ignorance

ADAPTATIONS

The Eagle has Two Heads
The Typewriter
The Apollo de Bellac
The Rabbit Race
Beauty and the Beast
The Trojan Women

EDITIONS

The Selected Writing of Mahatma Gandhi
The Poems of Ben Jonson
The Songs and Satires of the Earl of Rochester
Dante: De Vulgari Eloquentia

AUTOBIOGRAPHY

All Men are Islands
Obsessed
How to Make Enemies

Other Works by Ronald and Rose Marie Duncan

Where I Live
The Ward
Mr and Mrs Mouse

Ronald Duncan

SELECTED POEMS
1940-1971

Selected and introduced by Rodney Blumer

Rebel Press

First published in 1978 as a Selection
by the Rebel Press, Welcombe, Bideford
Devon

Designed, printed & distributed by
The Compton Press Ltd.
The Old Brewery, Tisbury, Salisbury
Wiltshire

Acknowledgments are made to
Faber & Faber Ltd. & Rupert Hart-Davis Ltd.
for their kind permission to reprint

ISBN 0 900615 17 6

Contents

Editor's Note

Ronald Duncan's first volume of poems was published in 1940, his most recent in 1976. The aim of this brief selection, in which the poems appear in chronological order, is to give some indication of his extraordinary range, from the simple to the complex, from the dramatic to the pastoral. Some influences must be mentioned: those of Gandhi, with whom he lived and worked in 1937 and whose prose work he has selected and edited for publication, of his lifelong friend and sometime publisher T. S. Eliot, and of Ezra Pound, from whom he learned the importance of form. It was Pound who in the '30s read him his translation of Cavalcanti's "Donna mi priegha", and ever since then the strict form of the Canzone has played a central part in his output, dominating his work in the '40s and '50s and threaded through the verse plays that first won him fame.

He sees form as a necessary discipline, as "an antidote to the slush of *Transition* and *New Directions* free verse which swamped the '30s and '40s. I saw the Canzone as the equivalent of the double fugue: infinitely more intricate than a sonnet or sestina". Determined to avoid what Pound called "subjective hosannas", Ronald Duncan deliberately chose to don the straitjacket of form to intensify that directness of communication which is the chief characteristic of his writing, whether in verse or prose.

Throughout the '60s, indeed for 12 years, Ronald Duncan worked on a five part poem of epic proportions entitled "Man". Deeply disturbed by the artificial chasm between the arts and the sciences – a chasm excavated only in the last 150 years or so – he resolved to try and bridge it with a full scale biography of the species to which he belongs, to try and view man within the context of the 4,000,000,000 odd years of earth's history. This involved a massive voyage of self-education in physics, geology, biology and anthropology, during which he came to believe that there was "more poetry in the laboratory than in the literary magazine". The poem is now finished, and has been published. The fact that its worth has been recognized by scientists the world over rather than by fellow poets is taken, I believe, as something of a compliment. Otherwise, it has either been ignored or wilfully misunderstood, though there is no doubt in my mind that it will come to be recognized as one of the weightiest artistic achievements of the 20th century.

Ronald Duncan has worked in a coal mine, been arrested as a vagrant, founded a commune, served a brief term in gaol, been a practical pacifist—indeed fulfilled most of the conditions expected of a poet by society. For 40 years he has lived in North Devon, on a stretch of coast line that has remained miraculously unspoiled. From near the 13th century mill that is his home you can scan the skyline without seeing anything that has been made by man. Despite occasional forays to London of varying lengths, whether to supervise the staging of his plays, to lunch with Eliot, to be instrumental in founding the English Stage Company, but studiously to avoid literary junketings – not for nothing did Pound dub him "the lone wolf of English letters" – Devon has always been and always will be his home. The huge granite cliffs, their feet pounded by Atlantic rollers, and the hidden valleys that creep inland invisible from roads or defunct railways, have inevitably left their mark on his work, notable as it is for its strength, directness and complete lack of artifice.

R.M.B.

THE RAPE OF LUCRETIA

A libretto set by Britten

Interlude

MALE CHORUS

Tarquinius does not wait
For his servant to wake,
Or his groom to saddle,
He snatches a bridle

And forcing the iron bit
Through the beast's bared white teeth,
Runs him out of the stable,
Mounts without curb or saddle

The stallion's short straight back,
And with heel and with knees
Clicks his tongue, flicks his whip,
Throws the brute into mad gallop.

Impetuous the powered flanks,
And reckless the rider;
Now the Prince and Arab steed
Bend as one for both are speed.

Hear the hoofs punish the earth!
Muscles strain, tendons taut,
Tail held high, head thrust back,
All's compact, nothing's slack.

See, the horse takes the bit
Between his teeth, now no rein
Can impede or stop him.
Yet the Prince still whips him.

Now who rides? Who's ridden?
Tarquinius, the stallion?
Or the beast, Tarquinius,
In both blood furious

With desire impetuous
Burns for its quietus;
With speed flame through sweat and dust
The arrow flies straight as lust.

But here they cannot cross.
Turn back, Tarquinius;
Do not tempt the Tiber:
Try to swim this river!

Stallion rears, hoofs paw the stars,
The Prince desires, so he dares!
Now stallion and rider
Wake the sleep of water

Disturbing its cool dream
With hot flank and shoulder.
Tarquinius knows no fear!
He is across! He's heading here!
Lucretia!

Lullaby

She sleeps as a rose upon the night
And light as a lily that floats on a lake
Her eyelids lie over her dreaming eyes
As they rake the shallows and drag the deep
For the sunken treasures of heavy sleep.
Thus sleeps Lucretia.

Epilogue

FEMALE CHORUS

Is it all? Is all this suffering and pain,
Is this in vain?
Does this old world grow old
In sin alone?
Can we attain
nothing
But wider oceans of our own tears?
And it, can it gain
nothing
But drier deserts of forgotten years?
For this did I
See with my undying eye
His warm blood spill
Upon that hill
And dry upon that
Cross?
Was that all loss?
Are we lost?
Answer us
Or let us
die in our wilderness. Is this all? Is this it all?

MALE CHORUS

It is not all. Though our nature's still as frail
And we still fall,
And that great crowd's no less
Along that road,
endless and uphill;
yet now

He bears our sin and does not fall
And He, carrying all,
turns round
Stoned with our doubt and then forgives us all.
For us did He
live with such humility;
For us did He
die that we
might live, and He forgive
Wounds that we make
and scars that we are.
In His Passion,
Is our hope.
Jesus Christ, Saviour, He is all! He is all!

(*The lights fade on the mourning group. Only Female Chorus and Male Chorus remain lit.*)

MALE AND FEMALE CHORUS

Since Time commenced or Life began
Great Love has been defiled by Fate or Man.
Now with worn words and these brief notes we try
To harness song to human tragedy.

(*The house curtain slowly falls.*)

CANZONE

(from *This Way to the Tomb*)

ST ANTONY

To live is to remember,
to die is to forget;
Present existence
is all reminiscence,
memory
Of our imperishable soul's past journey
woven in and out of time
As strands which never sever,
we thread death to birth and get
New feet for the old dance;
then, in a trance
of illusory
And receding imagery
dream and renew the climb

Back to the mind of God where our deathless soul began
And knew oblivion.
Back from death to infancy,
Back from birth to our last exequy
over and over climb to where
We came from and return when He, remembering us.
recalls us, and pities our despair.

Behind the forgotten poem lies the remembered vision.
And this song
which I sing in a bewildered ecstasy
Seeks its first silence with loud urgency.
I know who you are;
And you, in recognizing me, prove that our souls
remember by forgetting self in prayer.

BERNARD (*Kneels*).

Father.

ANTONY

Man's soul is virtue;
his nature evil.
Full of self, brutal,
material,
visible
And therefore perishable.
But the ageless soul survives
In so far as it stays pure
And sustains its vigil
And remains unnatural,
invisible,
indissoluble,
thus immortal,
the ghost of God walking through our lives.
It is easier to question than accept the answer
And there are
those who deny the spirit
Because they cannot weigh it.
But beauty is immeasurable
And we perceive it through the projection of our soul's
sad eyes.

If we were nothing, but fleshy vehicles of small desire
Masked with fear,
What in us would define desire's limit
Restrain the voluptuary, make the hermit?
Nor can you say the soul's inseparable
From the body and is to it as harmony to the lyre,
death silencing the whole.

BERNARD

And, Father is the soul immortal?
Is there life after death?

ANTONY

Everything must renew,
nothing living is immutable.
The fairest flower
falls in the hour
and becomes dust
As the proudest Emperor must
and leave the purple canopies of Rome
For the sepulchre's strict curfew.
Nor are the dead unchangeable;
Death's solid splendours
life devours
through the soil's lust
The seed takes, and the thirsty roots thrust,
– and as a cabbage, Kings re-enter Rome.

If the wheel did not revolve and all life upon this earth
Died in death
and did not quicken,
Nor reawaken,
and the severed lay forever fallen
And the buried body were forever broken,

Then in time all life would lie absorbed in greedy death
And no birth
from the tomb could quicken
Nor from the womb awaken.
From Life our death is taken,
From death our life is drawn. So with our souls. Amen.

THE EAGLE HAS TWO HEADS

(from Act Three)

QUEEN

Great love is great in agony
To it, pain is peace;
    Those who are born slaves are free
Compared to us
    who are imprisoned in this tyranny.

STANISLAS

Those who are burnt to death
Never know this cruel flame
    consuming all within, so pitiless
        is desire.

QUEEN

    And those who freeze to death
Do not feel so cold
    as those who love and then, unloved,
Feel, as they grow old.

STANISLAS

Oh God, is there no mercy
For those who love?
    Is this the punishment
Or, is this the sin?
    Then let the bubble of creation burst
I shall not care so long as there is left
    Above the rubble of the world
Her eyes at which I stare
    through which I see,
        and seeing know;
Now is eternity.

(*Pause. The Queen lowers her veil. Then continues in a whisper.*)

QUEEN

Oh God, deliver me from this pit
Of great personality and small habit
And deliver me from custom and conduct
And blast my enormous castle
Of little lies.
Let me know that it is often prudent to be foolish,
And often modest to be naked.
And force my lips to say
That which I do not wish to say :
Stanislas, I love you.

STANISLAS

I love you.

Now I know I could kill you
So as not to lose you.

QUEEN

Lay your head on my lap.
My hand is on your head;
Your head is on my knees.
How heavy it is.
I loved you when you first came into my room :
Yet I was ashamed.
I loved you when you were exhausted,
When your hand fell on the floor like a stone :
Yet I was ashamed.
I loved you when you insulted me :
Yet I was ashamed.
I love you now,
Now I am not ashamed.

STANISLAS

Some dreams can be so real
They waken those who dream them.

We are the dreams of a man who sleeps so soundly
He does not know he dreams. We must let him sleep
And whisper lest we wake him.

THE QUEEN

Oh, my beloved,
What is love?

STANISLAS

The water that falls in the river,
Is love.

THE QUEEN

Oh, my beloved,
What is love?

STANISLAS

The river that flows to the sea,
Is love.

THE QUEEN

Oh, my beloved,
What is love?

STANISLAS

The river that's lost in the ocean,
Is love.

THE QUEEN

Oh, my beloved,
What is love?

STANISLAS

The swimmer who drowns in this river,
Is love.

HYLAS

(libretto for Britten)

I *Canzone*

THE ARGONAUTS

Through the blue waves
we Argonauts row :
In out;
In out,
oars bending,
Backs straining;
Our helmsman seeking the Golden Fleece-
Our steersman dozing; whilst we sweat like slaves
moving slowly over the unending waves, as we row :
In out;
In out;
wrists aching;
Backs breaking :
When, oh ! when will our Timesman's hammer cease
And we see Pegasae again ?

JASON

Not till I, Jason, son of Aeson, hold that Golden Fleece
Shall we cease
Or turn our course from Colchis.
Will you a crew of fifty heroes
turn back to Pegasae again ? Will Orpheus ?
Or you, Heracles, would you return and leave my
throne usurped by Pelias ?

HERACLES

Hylas is weak . . .

JASON

But Heracles is strong ! . . .

HERACLES

As strong as Hylas! . . .

JASON

For love is weak!

HYLAS

Peace!
From Heracles' vow Heracles knows no release;
And though my lips bleed from thirst, as a chrysalis
I can lie in his cool shadow till we reach Colchis,

THE ARGONAUTS

Now our prow lifts like Pegasus
As Heracles' strength is doubled by Hylas' weakness.

II

ORPHEUS

And through the sultry night
we rowed into the sullen dawn;
A merciless sun
vaults the horizon;
a heat mist rises,
Its brief moisture teases
our fierce thirst, as our Timesman's hammer beats
The brazen brass of light
Till it's as thin as a shadow on a lawn;
And the drunken sun
reels to the horizon
and spills his dregs of wine and leaves
Darkness as our mistress again,
and the night breeze our silken sheet.

HERACLES

What falls more softly than the petals of a rose? These eyelids
On Hylas' tired eyes.
And where is there a violet
Petalled as delicate
As these frail veins set in his golden skin
So cool, so smooth, sweeter than jasmin?

HYLAS

Oh Heracles, it is better that I should die
Of thirst than you should try
to row the Argo all alone and set
Yourself against the gods and fret
Your strength against their cruel will; for when
The gods see we mortals love like gods, they are
jealous, and punish us for that immortal sin.

III

THE ARGONAUTS

And our prow lifts like Pegasus
    As Heracles' strength is desperation's doubled
By Hylas'
    weakness;
        But when the timid deer of light
Had drunk and drained the quiet pool of night
  Our Helmsman saw and seeing cried . . .

HELMSMAN

Land ! Land !

JASON

So we turned course towards the Island of Cios
  And our thirst flamed in our throats as we struggled
Against the shore's pitiless
  breakers and the tide's duress;
    Then Heracles threw all his weight
And pulled with all his might
  breaking his oar as the Argo touched the untrodden
    sand.

ORPHEUS

Heracles lept from the boat to fetch water for the boy
  Hylas
And the crew of Heroes –
                    But Jason stopped him ! . . .

JASON

                    Heracles – is this
How Heracles breaks his promise ?
  You swore not to leave this boat till I returned to Greece
Bearing the Golden Fleece !

HERACLES

Hylas is weak . . .

JASON

But Heracles is strong ! Come back and mend your oar !
Let your boy Hylas
Bring water to the strong hero who is his frail shadow . . .

ORPHEUS

And Heracles kept his promise
And climbed back into the boat saying farewell to Hylas . . .

HERACLES

Not vows but your beauty binds me yet your love is my release.
Whilst you are away I, like a galley slave, shall be chained to anxiety –
thirsting only for your lips and seeking your eyes,
which like a cool, secret well, contain all that is my peace.

IV

ORPHEUS

The Island stands like panic
reared out of the sea's calm mind.
Its steep cliffs are
hideous as fear.
And as the boy began to climb the heroes all
Looked away dreading his certain fall.

HYLAS

But with bleeding knees and broken hands I found
A crack in the volcanic
rock and up this crawled to where sun-drenched
lizards sprawled and blind
Heavy-lidded bats were
as lepers hung over
an ivy-covered well.
And as I looked into its water I heard the Naiads call:

NAIADS

Hylas! Hylas! Oh lovely Boy!

HYLAS

And as I drank, in music was I drowned!

A NYMPH

Hylas, oh lovely supple boy, kneel down and slake
Your hot thirst, take
Our cool water to your lips, drink deep; then in our
shade, sink down and sleep; for, as you drink us
We of your loveliness
may drink, and steep your image in our eyes.

CHORUS OF NAIADS

Just as an indolent willow
Leans into its shade so does our song seek Hylas for its
echo.

HYLAS (*who is now* ECHO)

And as I drank, in music was I drowned!

ORPHEUS

As night fell, Hylas had not returned, so Jason said:

JASON

We can wait
No longer. We must take
the tide!

ORPHEUS

Then, Heracles leapt from the boat and promised us . . .

HERACLES

If you will only wait till I find Hylas
For that boy is all my strength; I will then lift the
Argo from the shallows.

ORPHEUS

And as we left we heard his call:

HERACLES

Hylas! Hylas!

ORPHEUS

And the indifferent cliff mocked him with dead echo.

V

HERACLES

How lonely is that moment
when we are lost from those we love;
It is as though
we'd died and go
like urgent ghosts which sudden grief has sped
Up the unending cypress avenues of the dead
dragging our heavy hearts – for hearts are heavier
when they are left behind
Just as dreams are lighter when they are with us before
our sleep is spent.
Now through tear-blind eyes, I seek the image of my
love;
Each form, his shadow;
each sound, his voice, his echo.

ECHO

Hylas! Hylas!

HERACLES

And as the wind whispered with his voice I called: Hylas!
Hylas!
Then followed, or was led
To a quiet well that shouted with the cry within my mind.

And as his voice rose from the silent water and called:

ECHO

Hylas, oh Hylas!

HERACLES

And as I called:
Hylas! Hylas! And with dumb grief stumbled seeking
His shadow in the might I heard the Argonauts calling:

CHORUS OF ARGONAUTS

Heracles! Heracles!

HERACLES

And thus was I caught
Between his echo and my vow and in wild sorrow sought
The secret well again, watching them row away as echo answered:
Hylas! Hylas! as I called.
So, as if to hear his voice, I cried my own name;
then as I listened to the echo calling:

ECHO

Heracles! Heracles!

HERACLES

It was as if sweet Hylas was in my arms crying
My own name. And thus I stayed and cheated grief of sorrow,
For our love is as immortal as undying echo . . . Hylas! Hylas!

CANZONE

I

Love like a dog barks
at the heel of my leisure,
yaps, teases my schemes,
and all my dreams,
brings all straight,
wherever they graze or wait,
even my blood runs to her
And her live eyes mark
the quick strength and measure
of this heart which seems
to beat extremes,
loves then hates,
is never moderate,
changeable as the weather.

And what her wet lips say softly, her eyes ignore,
and therefore
there is division in her state
making a quick debate,
and she does nothing,
and so allows him to serve her there, and bring

To her luminous womb an impatient emperor
who is more
than anxious to inherit his estate
before he abdicates;
while I on her smooth skin
press grateful lips, then bite my suffering.

II

And behind her head
stands our patient ancestry
ghosts, all our forebears,

they wait and stare
inactive,
whilst we in furious joy, live,
and allow them their release,
through our veins and bed;
for the child we make gaily,
runs to a tomb where
eyes mouth and hair,
the dead give
their representative
for a period, a lease

Of searching, like haphazard travellers
who never
know their way and are all fugitives
from their objective,
which is the womb and the grave, where
we at last reach our first and second mother.

And here she lies like a graceful river
and now her
hand moves and is restive,
a restorative,
and her thighs' sepulchre
yield new relics for her breasts' cool cloister.

III

Now a hospital
with lawns and flowers and bees,
and the loud silence
of slow suspense,
and anxious
visitors timidly curious,
and laughter from the kitchen
falls like a cymbal
of a server's sneeze;

then time's indifference
                is most intense,
minutes are ponderous,
                and this and that's an omen,
Till a bell perforates the corridor,
and a door
    opens and is shut on us,
and brisk nurses without fuss
                                bring bowls of water;
she tugs at a towel : she groans like a heifer;

Till it lies wet, on her thigh
                                she sweats from labour;
and they pour water
                                and smear its rigorous
limbs with numerous
                                ointments; its murmurs,
and missing the warm womb, cries in a temper.

IV

Whose birth is this and
                        whose death is this, in this
birth my death and she,
                the child, is she,
                        my shadow
and I her son's embryo?
                        Whose immortality
whose eyes and whose hand
    whose metamorphosis?
My father's? Is he,
                        through her, set free
from photos
    and from death's packed depot,
                    set to dance in her jeu d'esprit?

From his unmarked standard grave on which a cactus
    grew
and a few
    weeds waved pink flowers in the dry sirocco?
– her fingers are just so –
    and it's strange to look where
the child's eyes are and see one's grandmother.
This birth and any death makes an impromtu
interview
    with God, apropos
oneself; quid pro quo
    our terms, and His
where our minds are not but our hearts loiter.

V

In blind worm wisdom;
                    in river affluence
threshed grain generous,
            voluptuous;
                    as wheat falls,
sprawls on the floor liberal,
            or as seed to the soil's lust
falls, is not lost, comes
            back to its essence
to its first focus,
            and is vigorous,
                        prodigal:
wheat, man and woman, all
        must submit, so, which is just.

This I did. For there is no alternative
but passive
    sacrifice: to be the feast at the festival
the corpse at the funeral;
                else one sits chewing an idea,
an unconverted infidel to one's own dull dogma.

And so we love, in order that we may live,
and we give
   our life away. Now, I dare not close my eyes
for fear of seeing you
            nor open them to know you are not there
Maria ! Maria ! Maria !

Envoi

Now you can go, Canzone, in your new suit
   which I have made to your own strict measurement
and precise arrangement
            making my impatient heart fit
to your fixed limit;
      Those who dress to please the fashion
may turn their arse to you : kick it with passion !

BRIONY

Like a waterfall of wind
Her hair falls to her shoulder
Fair ? Oh, nothing is so fair
As this hair which curls in laughter

Round my hand, as light as light
Lies on the skin of water.
Where is there anything so fine ?
There, where the heather spider

Spins from the night's anatomy
A web to catch the stars
Which dawn lets fall as dew
As it mounts the sun, the tiger,

And through the blue pavilion
Rides where the honeysuckle spills
Its heavy secret scent
Into an evening indolent

And tires from picking passion fruit
And tying up the vines
Before the grapes' full lust
Bursts into black wine.

But there is no web woven
Nor head of lovely hair to hold
Time back from his pursuit
Or tether the mad equipage, age

Which tramples into dust
With its wrinkles and its rust
And its violence and its lust.
Dear Jesus, watch this child for me :
In loving her, I love Thee.

'AUBADE

(Suggested by the Provencal poem,
'Nereio' Canto III – Frederic Mistral)

MAN

Oh Rose Marie as you are my love
Put your head to the open window
And listen a while to my new song
Sung with sad joy and gay sorrow.

The sky is weeping tears of stars
And the wind has fallen
But the sky will dry its eyes of stars
When the night sees you.

GIRL

You move me less than the breeze the branches
My heart is no leaf to your song.
I am going to dive into the deep sea
And become a fish deaf to your song.

MAN

Oh Rose Marie if you make yourself
A fish under the deep wave
I will become a fisherman
And will fish for you.

GIRL

Oh but if you then become a fisherman
I will break your net with my wings
For I will then fly into the clear sky
And become a bird deaf to your song.

MAN

Oh Rose Marie if you make yourself
A bird above the green fields
I will become a bird hunter
And will hunt you.

GIRL

Yes, but if you become a bird hunter
You will not catch me in your snare
For I will land and become white clover
Lost in a field deaf to your song.

MAN

Oh Rose Marie if you make yourself
A grass in the thick meadow
I will become a shower of rain
And will fall on you.

GIRL

Yes, but if you become a shower of rain
You will not touch me with your drops
For I will become a cloud above you
And drift to a land deaf to your song.

MAN

Oh Rose Marie if you make yourself
A cloud drifting to India
I will become the lusty wind
And carry you.

GIRL

Very well, but if you become a gust of wind
You will not move me with your breeze
For I'll dissolve into the sun's warm rays
And melt the strings of your guitar.

MAN

Oh Rose Marie if you make yourself
A ray of the lovely sun
I will become a green lizard
And will drink you.

GIRL

Even if you become a salamander
You will not drink me with your lust
For I will become a mysterious moon
Lighting a witch cursing your song.

MAN

Oh Rose Marie if you make yourself
As naked and smooth as the moon
I will become the softest mist
And cover you.

GIRL

Well, even if you become a mist
You will cover the moon not me
For I will become a virginal rose
Untouched by your passionate song.

MAN

Oh Rose Marie if you make yourself
As open and free as the rose
I will become as the heavy dew
And lie on you.

GIRL

Go ! Lover ! Go ! and be off with you
Never ! Never ! will you have me
For I will become a gnarled old oak tree
And let the owls out-hoot your song.

MAN

Oh Rose Marie if you make yourself
As patient and still as a tree
I will become climbing ivy
And embrace you.

GIRL

And then let me tell you your arms will hold
Wood only wood, for to spite you
I will become a nun of St. Blas
And let the Mass silence your song.

MAN

Oh Rose Marie if you make yourself
As innocent as a white nun
I will become a chaplain
And confess you.

GIRL

And if you pass the doors of the convent
You'll find all the nuns around me
For I'll by lying in a winding sheet
Dead and the dead are deaf to song.

MAN

Oh Rose Marie if you make yourself
As yielding as a poor corpse
I will become the loving earth
And thus have you.

GIRL

Now at last I begin to believe you
And can see you are not joking
Here is my ring, and my door is open
The key to my heart is your song.

MAN

Oh Rose Marie you lift me from the dead
And look since seeing you
Only the stars, my Rose Marie,
Only they have fled.

SONG

Sedia-m'eu na ermida de San Simon
e cercaron-m'as ondas que grandes son,
au atendend' o meu amigo.
(*A Cantiga de Romeria by Meendinho*
Thirteenth century in Galician.)

I am kneeling in the chapel of Saint Simon,
Left by the tide of time to kneel alone.
My love's taken, and my heart is broken.

I am sitting in the chapel before the altar
Left alone by the tide turning all to winter
My love's taken, and my heart is broken.

Leaving me alone the tide has turned and gone
And night now dives to rescue the drowning sun
My love's taken, and my heart is broken.

And the drowning sun is drenching my last summer
And I too will die and go to my dead lover
My love's taken, and my heart is broken.

Now the drowning sun burns on the thin horizon
I will drown in the waves, in the tide. It is all done.
My love's taken, and my heart is broken.

THE MASON'S EPITAPH

He was neither prince nor politician,
no priest and no poet,
as the world knows them; but he was the man
to smooth stones, make each fit

straight to his quoin, and thus used less mortar
than contract masons waste,
with the next job as their present master,
in their slow toil of haste.

He worked no fixed hours, he just came and went,
carrying a jug of cold tea;
he'd stay till he'd used up all his cement,
then leave, with no temerity.

His work was such that each action contained
its own contemplation;
the more he gave his work, the more he gained
in strict meditation

on stones of infinite shape. He weighed
their neat rigidity.
Disciplined by working with these, he made
his own philosophy

which was as sound as any Analects,
– at least, in application –
all men and things to their own nature fit
with or without salvation.

'Larch is no good for a lintel,' he said,
'it warps young and rots old
true to its nature; and from friends,' he said,
'expect from friends their colds.'

Protected by these exact measurements
he spent his evenings home.
Freed from resentments and disappointment,
married – to be alone.

His wife, a woman of monotonous lust,
without one attraction.
He kept her pregnant, for he knew this must
assure some relaxation.

But to assess his solid character,
words do not weigh enough
Observe his walls, they maintain his nature;
see where he smoothed the rough

and how his beam's morticed. Then you will see
that civilization
exists where men work for posterity
and build from sheer passion

for durability. Prust built that way;
this shippen here proves it.
Living, he gave us this, and now we say:
He died to no profit.

PRACTICAL BALLAD

I

The site: choose a dry site.
Avoid building against a bank.
Leaning a building to a bank may save putting up a wall,
but dampness will seep through,
you'll see your mortar sweat,
you'll be feeding to keep your pig warm,
this way she'll not fatten, profitably;
you may get roast out of it, but no bacon.

The size: Floor eight foot by eight foot good –
and slope off to a gutter;
pig's urine swells the bean pods; cover from flies.
Height: that is your problem, your comfort,
for it is you who have to get in and fling the dung out,
at least once a week, this is most important.

Now is the time to be generous:
Throw the straw in, not one wad, but two, three, four –
The more straw the more dung
The more dung the more straw, eventually.
Oh, cover the pig she'll trample it.

As to the door, observe the stable and copy that;
Make it of seasoned wood that won't warp as mine did.
Don't buy a bolt get a smith to make one –
Strength, not ornament, is necessary.
And that goes for a pig-sty, and poetry.

STRATTON

(Act Three)

Soliloquy

Is she within it?
        No; however much we love
Or we are loved, we are alone
        And in our hearts are
Each separate as a stone.

What star is there
        In what unfathomed firmament
As lonely as man is
        Within his little heart?

What tiny shell
        In what enormous ocean
Lies so deep and dark
        As man beneath the puddle of his soul?

And, God, how maudlin man becomes
When he stands on the edge of the night
        And chucks the pebbles of his spirit
Into this pitiless pit
        Where echo is his answer.

If anyone could hear
        These secret fears of mine
How melodramatic they would sound.
        They'd say I was playing to the gallery.
So I am, but the gallery
        Is the indifference of the stars.
And from that reality
        Do not wake me back to dreams.

But if she is not within it,
        Then what is it that fills my heart?

It is fear
Like a maggot
In a nut:
Fear in my heart feeds on my heart
Till it leaves the shell
Empty as echo
Rinsed round about a bell;
And fear creeps out
And fat grief flaunts its wings;
Then our sons observe
the moth that was
the rags that were
All their fathers' hearts.

Thus the self, sensing its own mortality,
mourns for itself
And with self-pity
Anticipates its exequies in an inarticulate soliloquy
Before the vast yawn of night.
Yes, it's strange how night reveals
What light conceals
From the furtive rats which are our busy purblind eyes;

Why does this fear of death obsess me,
Making each day a slow march to the tombstone
At which I stand chief mourner and the corpse?
Is it because I see my son replacing me,
Time flowing to him,
Time bleeding from me . . . ?

Postscript to Act IV (not to be played)

Now will our old house stare
Through uncurtained windows
And its corridors ache
With remembered echoes;
And its great roof weep
For forgotten sorrows
        And the briar will replace the rose.

Industrious spiders
Will weave their tapestries;
And damp will embroider
The walls; as dust, gently
Falls, so lightly to cover
All in its secrecy
        And the briar will replace the rose.

Lawns will return to sedge,
Whilst weeds in their wantonness
Sprawl where the gates embrace;
As nettles lease all, docks possess all
And the wind collects its tithe
Destraining with ruthlessness
        And the briar will replace the rose.

For beauty now grows old
And loveliness decays,
And lips which once made lips
And eyes which once made eyes
And hands which have reached
Through centuries – all fall away
        And the briar will replace the rose.

For when the future's broken
Even the past's made barren;
Like an unplucked apple
On a leafless tree,
Its breast hangs shrivelled.
So let the blind wind laugh
Over our undecipherable epitaph
        And the briar replace the rose.

THE DEATH OF SATAN

(Act III)

SATAN

This is my last Will and Testament.
To those agnostics on the earth, worshippers of man and mediocrity,
I, Satan, hereby bequeath : equality, democracy and boredom,
Together with all my chattels and effects.
May they who've sought security, find it;
And, knowing that world without saint or sinner, good on evil,
Without excess for sin or art,
Without vitality for love or hate,
May they be without passion or piety, without poverty or charity.
To the men, I give opportunity without desire;
To the women, desire without fulfilment.
And may they breed and reproduce themselves,
Knowing birth without joy, and death without grief,
Till maggot eats maggot on the bare bone of the eroded earth
And the last expires with vomit.
But to you three who never believed in Heaven
Sufficiently to suffer any discomfort here in Hell, I bequeath :
Complete release from fear of retribution
Or hope of your redemption
I absolve you from all spiritual doubt
And leave you this material certainty : death.
Do not smile, you will not find that it's a quick escape to nothingness.
But a slow running down of your consciousness.

THE SOLITUDES

I

To my essential self – I sing –
Not to the I,
Man of the hat, coat and tie;
But to the me,
– coffee, muddle and misery.

2

Damn and blast you!
You behave like a pickpocket,
    or an absent-minded thief,
Raiding my sleep, when you don't even need my peace;
Stealing my heart, when you certainly don't want my
        love.

And all this done so arrogantly,
Done out of perversity, done out of sheer caprice,
Till I am undone, utterly besotted.

True, it's not your fault, you're not to blame:
Your sleight of hand's so practised, you don't even know
        you do it
And can't even think who it is
    who now complains bitterly –

I tell you beauty like yours should be punishable.
What right have your eyes to run up and down the street,
    creating this disturbance?
Your eyes are urchins; your lips, ragamuffins;
Everything about you is delinquent,
The whole of you gangs up
    to chuck pebbles through me.

But one day, Sir, I'll read the Riot Act to you
And claim back all my property, bit by bit, till I am whole again.
Till then, do not reform,
Treat me as an unguarded barrow loaded high with
        grapes,
Snaffle my peace of mind,
I value nothing which you do not
        take;
    Nor want these rags, the remnants which you leave.

3

To the lake of my aloneness
    No river flows
I am contained by mountains of my making.
Without wave I wait, wanting; but no heron
    comes and no swan goes.
The day delivers its indifferent glances;
Night passes, merely pausing to adjust
    an artificial rose.
I hold nothing but reflections;
I wake to my own shallows, I sleep soundly
    without repose.
Will no appled boy paddle in me?
Has no one a boat to float on me?
Must I quench my thirst, drink myself up
    and drown?

4

I would that my love should grow
    without a heart to feed upon;

I would that my heart should feed
    without a life to lean upon;

I would that my love should shine
    without an object, without a shadow;

I would that I should die within myself
    and live in my love for you and you and you
    as He did, yielding without possessing;
All other love is death,
    is death's amorous dissembling.

5

How leaf we are;
At first, all furled in separateness :
Peeping out with little vanities and hopes, also vanity;
Perhaps the last vanity, holding us to that green world
Out life shall be; believing ourselves
So individual, we all reach, being identical.
Shall the prodigal gardener weep ?

How leaf we are;
At last, all seared in brittleness
Curled up with tiny fears and hurts, also fears;
Perhaps the last fear, tethering us to that dry twig
Our life's become; then knowing that we are
Enumerable, we fall, being expendable, all.
The gardener is blind. He will not sweep.

How leaf we are
Like waves we do become; first urged, then merged.
That gardener is a fisherman;
That fisherman's asleep.

6

Why do You
laugh up Your sleeve of night
watching me, lonely, without You,
knowing You did not give me the sight to see You,
nor the strength to seek You?

What perverse pleasure do You find
playing cat and mouse and hiding from the blind
teasing the already torn and tormented mind?

And tell me: why did You have to give me eyes
which can only stare at her
and do not even glance at Thee?
Why did You lame me so
That I can run – to her
And cannot come – to Thee?

Cannot your divine and imprudent purpose be fulfilled
Unless I deny Thee so that You in Your turn can then,
forgive me?
Is my weakness indispensable to your strength?
Are we tied together – a tin can to a dog's tail?
It must be or You would not have made me so
That I can kneel to her
And will not bend to Thee;
That I can reach for her,
And cannot rise to Thee.

Or is it – oh, be it so –
That Thou made her for me
Knowing that by loving her, I'd come to Thee,
finding in her hands, Thy gentleness;
On her lips, Thy tenderness;
In her passion, Thy compassion?

It is so – oh do not take her from me –
    for see, Jesu, how I now run gaily to her, to Thee,
    Making this prayer a song to her, to Thee,
    an avowal without heresy.
    For as you know, Christ how well you know,
    When only love divides,
    Nothing is divided.

7

As wet lilac bruised with scent
Leans on the air indolent
And allows the wind to break
And permits the sun to slake
Its fierce thirst and quietus make

So you, my love, allow
And give, and add to it your vows
But do not seek a pledge from me.
Your vows give me my liberty,
Your eyes describe my tyranny.

8

You ask me to write a poem
Not because you like poetry
But because you like me,
And want to give something to me.

But because you are humble
(Modesty is another thing)
You do not offer me yourself, but myself
Knowing that is what I have lost or
absentmindedly mislaid,
And that it is something I shall not find again
In her, or her or you.
But might in moments like this to which you lead me
When I sit fishing in silence from a shoal of
quicksilver words
Which leap like salmon the instant that I look.
It does not matter where I look
at the petals of lilac falling to the grateful lawn;
at the tractor trailer burdened with its load of dung;
at her, or her or even you . . . it does not matter,
Anything which lives is poetry.

The restless swallows dive for flies, hunger is their song;
Watching them, I am, I find that self whenever I do not
belong.
So now I can give you this,
the self you give to me.

9

Because my eyes have stared
  So often at you
People looking at me
Should see your image impaled upon my face.

10

Dearest, do me a favour
 Treat me without mercy;
Let your cruelty
  Run free, so long as it runs over me
Love me as the wind loves
Waste me as water is wasted;
Ask and demand all from me, take the whole of
 me;
For only when you take that
  Can you give me, me.

II

Now that we love
Watch how the world conspires
To wreck, ruin and upset
this raft of our desires;
Now that we love
observe how Time will cheat
Us of that coinage
we do not counterfeit;
Yet now that we love
restrain all tears, just laugh;
Let joy be our purpose
a smile, our epitaph.

12

Dearest, since I cannot say why I love you
Let me tell you how I love you :
    I love you as a tiger loves its prey,
            intently, fiercely;
    I love you as the ivy loves its wall,
            closely, tenaciously;
    I love you as the lizard loves the sun
            completely, sleepily;
Dearest, if I must live without you,
It will not be life without you.
    Those who are born only once, die only once;
That is not our fate. But I am content in :
    the mercy of your being.

13

How can we be parted
Since we are no longer separate?
The train that conspires to take me from you
Will only take me to you:
You will be on the platform to greet me,
You will be in the taxi beside me.
Though I may speak to others,
I shall be talking to you;
Though I may look at others
I shall be looking for you.
When I walk I shall be walking towards you,
When I sleep I shall be lying beside you.
Because we are no longer separate
We cannot be parted. Yet I dread the world
That does not hold your eyes.

14

Dearest, it is no longer true
    For me to say I love you
Or that I desire you, though that was true
    A day or two ago, before you took me to yourself
        And from an individuality
        Made one identity
    To which we each are part and now belong.

For me to say I love,
Or that I still desired you
        Would be as tautological
        as tactful,
For we are in that state
In which there is no predicate or object.
Those who are separate
                                        love at lower rate.

15

Her moss of sleep upon the bark of night,
Her surf of dreams upon the tide of rest;
            So do we lie;
The lark of now into the song of sky;
Our leaf of love upon the tree of time;
            The wind blows, my blind hand knows
Sight, touching her breast.

16

As thrush, lark and linnet are
    So do my eyes rise,
Sing for the life in you
    Joyful at your being. Oh
                                                            be there

Where I am going, when I return to
    Be bark to my ivy
Tree to my climbing
    Be merciful
                                                            be here

Where my hope is, be there where my home was,
    Else I am lost, lonely as driftwood;
Be to the restless river, me
Clear pool of no purpose
                                                            be still

Peaceful as grass is, grow gently,
    Secretly beneath
Impetuous rain of me
    Be brave at my cruelty
                                                            believe

In my gentleness; forgive me for this,
    Forgive me for that. Contain my disparities;
Accept my extremities. Oh love me wholly, so
    Holy shall you
                                                            become.

17

All right, run off with you and go
But let me warn you, Madam, where you go, I am.
  The more you run from me,
  The more you run to me,
What you become, I am.

You seek another lover? Oh don't deny, or lie;
That's a useless thing to do to him
Who's made all these frailties his own.

But let me ask you: what quality has any other man
  Except he is not me, –
A somewhat negative attribute, you agree?

All he could be at his poor best
Would be to be deputy, understudy,
Plagiarising my hands, aping my eyes, parodying my lips,
And it's you who'll cast him as this stand in
To watch him try what I alone perform.

But I'm not jealous, give him encouragement, it's all you'll yield.
And all he'll take from you will be your tolerance,
Your patience and a yawn.

And don't think I'm being arrogant
I don't despise him. You misunderstand me there:
It is that I, being so sympathetic to his role
Am, he, at one remove.

And don't apologise; I have reached that point, philosophically,
  Where I perceive all lovers only labour and perform for me;
Extended thus, spiritually,
Insulated so, emotionally, I achieve
  Both the ease you denied me
And the anonymity that is yours.

18

There was no part of you
    my hands did not know.
Now separated,
    let the memory of my hands
Enfold your neck, your breasts, your thighs,
    gentle as petals fall
    or the wings of butterflies rise.

Be like a chrysalis contained by my fingers, encased by my touch :
Let the rude world stare at this robe you wear
    Dior could not copy it
    Paquin imitate it;
Go dressed in my hands, my desire the designer
    Clothed in this passion
    You are the height of fashion.

So flaunt the memory of my hands proudly
Till this blind glove with which I now write
Can undress you, and from your nakedness
Receive its flesh, its purpose and its sight,
Embroidering your skin in the fierce tattoo of night.

19

Oh my God with what agility
does jealousy
jump into a hot heart
and fit,
till it fills it,
or is, a great part.

And how strange it is that I myself
should from myself
make, riding her thighs
at speed
(or slow as love needs),
rivals which are his eyes

Unfocussed, yet in blindness seeing
all of being;
opaque, his opal eyes shew
sorrow,
it is as though,
my wrinkled son had said :
'I who am born was never dead' and said :

'There is no birth, death, joy or sorrow
I am not you,
nor are you me;
we are each free,
linked with no separate identity.

All is as water flowing endlessly
leisurely
over a smooth hard stone.
Only a thin skin,
pattern on the water, this, our own.'

20

Do me a favour, treat me with contempt:
Laugh at my poetry, say my last play's dull, a bore,
Not half as good as one I wrote before.
Find where my faith hides and what my ideals are –
or were, then ridicule them. Beg for my heart
And when I give it you
Bounce it casually on the floor –
No more!
That's not enough! Do more!

Make lonely my own home: rid me of sleep,
And if and when I do, play patience with my dreams,
Shuffle dexterously, mark the whole pack;
And when I wake, see that it's not from you.
Cheat me of purpose; deprive me of my wit,
Make me despise myself
Assure all my friends' derision –
No more!
That's not enough! Do more!

Cuckold me with a painter – anyone will do
For me, or you! Inform me of the day, the hour, the place
Make sure I hear the details – tell her
In secret, leave the salt to her: omit no item
Or dimension; do as all bitches do –
exaggerate one or two
brag it was better than before
No more!
That's not enough! Try more!

Find where I'm vulnerable, then stretch the wound.
Borrow my money – there's an idea for you!
Try breaking my pocket since my pride won't break
Then when I need the cash, say you gave it him!

You'd think that ruse would work, but if it fails :
Promise to dine with me; come late
No more !
That's not enough ! Much more !

Make me complain, then say you'll give him up,
Swear vows or try at least to produce a tear or two
Till I, to stop the flow, beg you to forgive
Me – for making you do what you did to me.
Now comes your chance; reconciled and grateful
I drop all my defence
Aim straight, wound where I am still raw
No more !
That's not enough ! Do more !

Betray me utterly. For that you'll need
Some new device; a mere fuck or two won't do.
Even when you admit that lapse was not
From weakness but deliberately done :
That your vow was false as the groans you faked
for him. No, any cunt
Can do that trick. Try something more :
Much more !
It's not enough ! Do more !

What could it be ? Where is a poet hurt ?
Ponder a while – what's made 'em bleed like hell
before ?
When digs into their pride and pocket failed ?
What drove da Falla mad, made Minton drink
Pushed poor Van Gogh till he removed an ear –
Or was it something else
Or more ? You'd know if it were that !
Think more !
That's not enough ! Think more !

Think what it was bust Schubert's mighty heart.
That's it. You're getting close! You're getting warm,
I see!
Yes; we all share the same sincerity.
So hunt out some token which I gave to you
Sell it. Tell what I told you through my eyes
In secret. Play it down.
Not just the moment, cheapen me
No more!
You've tried all that! Get more!

Get dentures loose, then henna up your hair.
Deflate your breasts, achieve a spotted thigh, be smug,
Be slovenly in your dress, shifty in your eye
Acquire indifference. Oh, for pity's sake,
Do these things which time will do to you –
For all the rest you've done
Yet I still love, as I have loved before
It's not enough?
Find more! Find more!

21

Murderers are merciful compared to me
    who with the same intention
    lacked their resolution
And failed, but not from kindness, I was never without cruelty
That you know; nor was it that I had no need, that I know;
For my peace, I had to put you to rest,
                    And so I tried
Several slow ways to kill you,
                    Yet you have not died.

You will remember my first attempt
    which lacked a dagger's courage
    or a poison's quick relief :
How I struck blindly where you were most vulnerable,
At your love, and where I knew you were undefended, because you loved.
I did not use a knife; my words were sharper
                    As I denied
My love and watched my words wound and saw you bleed
                    yet you have not died.

And at that failure, how I next sought
    to strangle what I'd weakened
    though it had not died, though I then sent you from me
And told her, and her and him that you meant nothing to me
Knowing they from friendship would tell you . . .
                    Christ ! how I lied
And tried to hide the wound you were that blossomed in my side
                    yet you have not died.

But out of perversity you have grown stronger
    as though you fed upon neglect
    and were nourished by starvation;
And so, at last, I brought you back again to see if familiarity would kill

What had only flourished when we parted. And how I next
Belittled what you gave me, and urged myself to continence
till you complied
And let me be as faithful to her as you remained to me,
yet you have not died.

Even though I then drove you to another
Hoping jealousy might do for me
What it had failed to do for you;
And how I then used to come and sit upon the bed where you had lain –
or should I say had lied?
Yet savoured your betrayal
pretending we were identified,
Managing to absolve myself of responsibility to you
yet you have not died.

But have become the mongrel at my side
I run from only to seek;
As a blind man, his guide,
So on you I relied; not for my existence, but for my being.
Of what use were my eyes unless they saw you? My hands
Unless they touched you? . . . That dependence
I abhorred, defied
And deliberately tried to hide from that unwanted bitch that dogged
my side
yet you have not died.

But lived a restful life within my restless sleep
So that all my dreams were webs
To catch you on the wing,
Or like busy streams pretending to turn from you
Only to flow to you. Peace was where you were, and you were in my
sleep
As I'm in yours . . . Thus do we two lie apart, but not
alone, certainly not divided
As night's tide

Turns and makes us wake to loneliness
Yet you have not died.

Though I have sought within this wilderness of thought
To murder what I loved,
Knowing that was suicide,
For we are what we love; but not mercy, self-survival
Now makes me keep you and your memory alive in me. And now I
have lain you in this verse

Live there after your life in me
when I have died
For, till then, there is no way
for you to die in me – though I have tried,
though you have tried.

22

If our ability to love
Can only be assessed by our capability to forgive, then my darling,
I must be grateful to you for teaching me the language,
Though I confess I've sometimes found it difficult
To articulate all the charity you earned
And was till now often dumb with resentment, bankrupt in my love.

The fault was yours; how could I learn to forgive
If you failed to confess ? I blame you there,
Your modesty and reticence made me backward
And my Elementary Love remained in the Remove,
Not knowing the tenses of maturity
Or the conjugations of your sex.

How could my love develop, if it
Had so little to forgive, and I was always the one
To be forgiven ? No wonder I remained
Still learning the alphabet
While you graduated from tolerance to indifference.

It was not kind of you to keep me illiterate for so long.
Knowing your virtue, taught me nothing but that I lacked it.
True, I admired you for yours; but since I thought you faithful to me,
Your virtue was something I left for others to forgive.

If I've been jealous it was because
I thought you were giving them lessons you denied to me.
That this was not the case, and they had nothing to forgive
Does not alter the fact that I now sit here for my examination
Without having had adequate preparation.

Your little perjuries were not enough
To teach me charity. Neither were your fits of envy
– I mean those of me – sufficient for my education;

Nor was your frigidity a fault to teach me
Anything but pity; and pity has no more to do with love
Than desire has with compassion.

You were of course quite generous to me
In your long deception : I thank you for that.
For if you had told me frankly at the time
That you had been unfaithful to me
I would have had nothing to forgive –
Except that more temptation had come to your door
Than I had often found in my gutter.

No, it was not your long deception
That is my present lesson. That's too easily understood,
Too easily forgiven. It's one thing to tell a priest –
But a husband tends to be more attentive
And less impartial as a confessor.

Besides which, as I know we sometimes
Hide the truth from those we love, not for our own protection,
But for theirs. That you did this to me,
Was no more than to quote me to my face;
And though I tend to resent my own faults seen in others,
– plagiarism flatters as the devil only knows.

And of course women have their own temerity,
They can't brag of their adulteries with effrontery,
They have to be secret in order to be kind; as Sweeny says :
Somebody has to pay the rent; and as that's not them
What else can they do but go on nourishing their indiscretion ?
Though the worm gnaws at their breast, they can always wear a bra.

No, your lies and adulteries give me as little to forgive
As your insensitivity did – or does.
And, of course, I know you would have been more honest
If I had been more understanding. To condemn a woman for her lies

Is as unreasonable as blaming a bird for its wings.
The best we could do would be to resent the fact that their flight
Is always more sustained than ours.

Similarly, I realise that you would have been more faithful
If faith had been more fashionable. And was I not
A leader of fashion – we'll not refer to taste?
For there to be forgiveness, there must be anger first;
And the more I hear, the more sympathy obtrudes.
Now what can I learn of love, if I've only fashion to forgive?

Even if you'd used your pretence of virtue
To double my sense of guilt, so that I had then become
Untrue to myself, as I had been untrue to you,
And if that had then made me abandon her
And loose my self-respect – even that I could easily forgive.

For when a woman helps a man to loose all self-esteem
She does him a greater favour than she knows
Or maybe she intends. Yes, even if you had done this to me
And made me lose a woman's love, that would have been a favour,
Certainly, nothing I could not forgive.

You claim that's what you did? Then it seems you are forgiven –
Poets, my darling, are born with love. I did not need your lesson.

23

Any man might miss
  Your lips or thighs, but I
Miss the slut, the shrew in you;
And hate this quiet peace which lacks your nasty tongue,
Bored with my bed too big without your bum.

Any man might want
  You for your charm, but I
Want the bitch, the nag of you;
And walk this slow evening so dull without your spite,
Sick of my thought, less you're distracting it.

Any man might love
  You for some part, but I
Love you whole, even your heart,
In which I am contained, though I've not entered it,
– Or so you say sometimes, only because you wish to give it me again.

24

Just as I used
    to wear your old sweater
Preferring the rag that was yours
    because it was yours
to anything that was mine,

So now I wrap myself
    within this loneliness
Preferring this fact and its cause
    because it is yours
to any dream that was mine.

25

I have at last come to terms
    with your curtains;
I can now look at them for what they are;
They no longer hurt me because you made them.

And slowly I am making my peace
    with your garden.
I see your bulbs now like fingers through the weeds
They make me sad, but it is a sadness I am learning to accept.

It is your pile of flat stones
    by the gate;
Those you dragged bravely up from the bed of the stream
To make a path with, it is that which is so belligerent
        and will have me on the run.

26

Dearest, be ruthless :
   give me more love
Or give me more disdain;
Abandon your pose of pity,
Stop teasing me, show me contempt;
Love of our intensity
                                   should be violent to be tender :
It's your kindness that is unkind.

Dearest, be generous
   give me more love
Or give me more despair
Either yourself or your emnity :
Stop liking me, be cruel and hate;
Love of our intensity
                                should be savage to be gentle;
It's your kindness that is unkind.

27

Words are a net;
Feeling, the water escapes through the meshes
I fish for silence.

AIR RAID

Like skulls with all their fears still there
The houses squat around the square,
And through their broken windows stare
Into each other, with fixed despair.

In the hall at No. 21
Where my aunt received anyone who was somebody,
A white glove like a severed hand lies on the floor.
Her 'phone rings; but nobody answers her trunk call from Hades
To tell Stone where Mr. Ronald sits
At dinner – between two corsaged, safe ladies.

Now rats are residents at Embassies,
Cockroaches call, and mice are prodigal:
This war does more than spoil her Season
It's quite upset her Peke's poor reason.

And now the drunken staircase climbs the peeling walls
Into the salon where bats bleat madrigals.
Across the hearth two marble cupids sprawl.
Dust settles quietly, inheriting it all.

HELOISE TO ABELARD

So, you wish me to withdraw!
  I will not; I will do no such thing. Even if I could.
I would do no such thing.

You ask me not to shew my love for you
  Because you see no hope for us in it;
There never is any hope for those who love:
  But I don't want hope: I want love.

Why do you write as though our emotions
  were something we could control and use?
If they were controllable they would not be emotions.
  but thoughts.
To seek a reason four our feelings
  is like seeking a reason for God.
I am as you know a poor logician
  and a worse theologian:
But I postulate this:
  that what is, in essence,
Needs no reason or justification
  other than its being.

Love is, or it is not:
  it requires no purpose nor destination:
But is, of itself; sufficient in itself
  it needs no hope, it has no cause;
And if suffering is part of love,
  then I am content to suffer.

The reason for your pain
  is that your pride prevents you
From submitting to your own nature
  which is part of God.
Why can you not, beloved,
  accept your love and the suffering which it is?

I suspect that you ask me to be constant
        to my devotions, and not to you,
Only because you feel guilty
        that you are the object of a passion
You do not reciprocate.
        Are you not using piety
To mask your coldness towards me?
        Will not your conscience be lightened
If I depend less on you?
        But I will do no such thing!
You say you wish to save your soul:
        Let me confess I only wish to save our love –
For a woman, that is the same thing.

If it's a sin to love
        then I am sinful and unrepentant,
Worse: grateful for my capacity to sin.
        Did you not yourself teach
In your great Treatise: 'Sic et Non'
        that, if the soul of the world is to come to its full creation,
We must apprehend its reality completely?
        Did you not write
That unless evil is unique and is alone outside the Divine plan
        Some purpose must be inherent in both good
And evil –
        both in the body and the spirit alike?

Now is the philosopher confused:
        treating me as a thing apart from my universal nature,
which is my reality,
        forgetting my love which is me, which is you.
Oh shame on you!
        What sort of God is this we worship
Who having created us wholly
        stipulates that we should be grateful

For the gift of life in part?
    Is not that God, a mad God,
If having made me woman
    He insists that I should deny my nature
As you seek to deny yours?
    I cannot learn to love Him
Unless he allow I first love you.
    Love is not divisible.
For He himself is not divisible.
    Would you have me believe in a God
Who wants you to worship Him with your hands but not
your feet,
    who wants your prayers, but not your passion?
If such a jealous God wants to take you from me
    Then I hate Him,
He is no God to me!
    I tell you, if that is the way He loves
Then I can compete with Him.
    Now hear my heresy
It is a confession without penitence:
    I love you wholly;
And behind that word, is my hand;
    And behind that hand is my blood.

    I was seventeen when you first took me to you –
– Oh where is that time fled? –
    I was a girl; your love made me a woman,
It has been a slow painful growth;
    I am grateful for the pain,
The growth I now give back to you,
    hold it in your hands like a poppy,
Learn how this woman learned to love
    And do not turn away, not crush the petals
You yourself created.
    For this is how I love:

You, for your kindness; you, for your cruelty;
    You, for your gentleness; you, for your violence;
for the poet that you are;
    for the man that you are not,
for the child that you were,
    for the corpse you will become.
I love both your body and your mind
    Not only the chiselled sinews of your neck
but the sweat from your armpits,
    I love your vision that kindles
and your lack of vision that makes me want to take you by
                                                            the hand.
    If this is not how God loves.
It is how I love.
    I believe we are most holy
When we become most whole.
    And if God does not love like this,
I will make love my God.
    No, I will not withdraw!

You will see that this letter has been torn across:
    Some I have written without modesty
And that will stay with me, where there is no shame.
    But that which I send here
Has, as you'll see, been written in anger
    written from jealousy
I give you the gift of my anger
    the gift of my jealousy.
They are wings for my love
    on which I fly to you.

EASTER LULLABY

Lord Jesus once was a
child like thee
Yet there has been no
other.
Lord Jesus laughed once
just like thee,
For Mary's delight, as
you delight me.
Weep, child, weep for
Jesus' Mother.

Lord Jesus once had hair
like thee.
His could have been no
softer;
With skin as smooth and a
mouth like thee,
And eyes that had wept
before they could see;
Sleep, child, sleep for Jesus'
Mother.

Lord Jesus once had toys
like thee,
Throw, child, throw your
ball higher;
And hands that His Mother
kissed like me,
Hands that my hands
nailed to a tree;
Weep, child, weep for thine
own Mother.

ASCENSION

It was not that I raised myself to Him
  But that He reached down for me.
And during that time, after they had found the tomb empty,
I was among them.
  Seeing me, Mary Magdalene embraced me.
  'Do not cling to me thus,' I cried
  'While I am still a man.'
  'What a man loves, he does become.'
  For two days, I wept at her grief for me.
  For two days I walked beside her
    sharing no burden, casting no shadow
  It was not that I had risen from the dead
    but love had not died in me.

Then, as I watched them disperse
back to the nets, the loom, and the last
  from which I'd called them,
I saw their disappointment that the Kingdom I had brought,
had not been the Kingdom they had sought,
The only crown I wore,
Scratched my forehead badly;
The only throne I knew,
Pattered on four little hooves.
And as I watched them and walked with them I wondered
  whether I had not sinned greatly :
  by burdening their innocence with a vision they couldn't share;
  by confusing them, setting father against son, son against father.

I stood for a moment observing Peter
  dexterously mending the mesh in his net,
And in that moment I saw the whole tapestry of tears
  which I had woven :
Two thousand years, with less love at the end of it;
And I saw Charity's long crusade of savagery;

Tolerance turning to bigotry and faith to the thumbscrew.
And seeing all this and foreseeing all that
With so few, so few, not even twelve to understand,
I walked on, leaving no footprints save in my remorse.
  The earth I loved had hands.
  It held me by the feet.

Then in the garden, that garden, I suffered a second agony;
  their nails, gentle to these nails,
  their cross light to this cross: the realisation
That I should not have projected the struggle within me
  but should have lived it internally:
  denied myself, betrayed myself, judged myself and thus given man
  that love he could not give me: a compassion
  beyond the Passion.
That was the thought which crucified me.
Forgive me, for I knew what I had done.

It was not that I raised myself to Him
  but that He, in great mercy, reached down for me.

THE GIFT

Since she whom I love
    has a gift for jealousy;
I – a talent for adultery,
We reached that point where
We kept our friends in conversation;
Lawyers in fees, and ourselves
In something that passed for anger,
But was more like grief.

Now I see I must learn to love
    her jealousy :
    it being part of her,
And hope that she can love me
    for my adultery.
But this she's done. This she's done.
Could it be her jealousy was a gift,
    A gift to me ?
We have begun. It is not done.

FOR A DYING WOMAN

She lies propped up by pillows,
Her pink hands clutch the sheet like a bird's feet in the snow.
Her eighty years heavy in her eyes,
Shawled loosely round her shoulders.
They say she is frail. I do not see frailty.
What rock is there strataed in darkness
Diamond with strength of will?
Or where is there a river flowing
So that its tide can ebb and flow at its own volition?
Compared to her a gale is listless
And every star is impotent, for every star is dumb.
Life does not lie in mobility,
But only in consciousness.
I do not send her flowers, but this
    her own life that is in her,
the articulated point in a blind and dumb universe.

MAN

PART I

CANTO NINE

ERAZE

$$U\frac{238}{92} \rightarrow Pb\frac{206}{82} + 5He\frac{4}{2}$$

Roams back the rose. Through what wild age
roams back the rose?
1 gram of uranium transforms into .865 of lead, .133 of helium
and .002 radiation.
A natural process, neither accelerated nor slowed,
by either temperature or pressure:
A natural process, nothing to do with fission
no neutron added to split the nucleus
A natural disintegration, instability of isotope.
Therefore, each year 1.5×10^{10} of any mass of uranium
Decays, breaks down, is converted.
From which data,
Age of oldest rocks of earth:
5 or 6,000 million years.
That is, minimum time, not allowing for
period of cooling, of solidification.
Use of actinium or thorium as atomic clocks
yield similar time scales
At variance with Archbishop Ussher's statement
that the Earth was created on Sunday 23rd October 4004 B.C.

PART II

CANTO FIFTEEN

ARCHEAN (2)

Ribbed with iron, fleshed with rock,
the blind Earth turned within its envelope of darkness,
Beneath a shroud : atmosphere of ammonia, methane and steam
through which the fingers of light could not penetrate;
Oceans of lava groping in darkness,
mountains wading through perpetual night.

Not till the Earth cooled, the fumes condensed,
could the sun stab with that mercy which is light;
Then the first rain fell upon the still scalding rocks
and the steam put out the light again;
And it rained for ten thousand years,
not night and day, but throughout the night,
For light could not penetrate the cloud
which caused the rain, which caused the steam,
Which kept the earth dark for this desert grained with years.

Then, where there had been tides of molten rock,
one scalding ocean of water
Enveloped the fractured Earth.
Great waves swept beneath a starless sky
And never found a shore.
No life in the seas
Or secret beneath them. No movement
but the wind combing the wave's mane
As those eyeless wild horses
stampeded over the prairies of night,

Dragged by a tide
drawn by an invisible moon: night,
Heavy night lay like a stratum of slate
over that sterile sea.

Then once upon a dream, a nightmare of nights ago,
the seas cooled, the clouds of steam dispersed,
And the sun daggered the horizon again, and the light,
the light entered its inheritance,
Walking with white feet over the silent waters,
Sowing the seed of life
Until the great belly of the Earth was pregnant:
All from water
All from light.
That is where the dream began,
In the microbe, in the man . . .

No, this won't do at all. Not at all. This sort of rhetoric
might pass for poetry, or something like poetry,
Not for sense. My image of a molten earth
with an atmosphere of ammonia, methane and steam,
Unlikely. More probably, the earth was cool
when it condensed, then only slowly
Heating up from internal pressure, nuclear fission;
no evidence of CH_4 or NH_3.
Though these gases shroud Jupiter and Saturn
as spectrometer analysis proves, it does not follow
They were present on the earth, in spite of Oparin-Urey theory,
or Miller's experiment in synthesising two amino acids
By passing an electric discharge through them.
A similar base for protein might possibly emerge
From other gases struck by lightning . . . Back to your books.
As to the steam, and your oceans of scalding water, you dolt,
where precisely do you think that came from?
Picture of a molten Earth bandaged by steam,
salved by water, most convenient,

Given the water.
There could have been no steam without water,
No water without steam . . . More probably, then :
the primitive Earth cool,
entirely dry,
with no atmosphere,

Certainly no oxygen,
possibly some nitrogen, mainly carbon dioxide,
Emerging from interior gassing,
but no water. Then how,
From where, did it appear ? Back to your books. But which books ?
Hogbom, Arrhenius ? A hint in Herbert Spencer . . .
Extraordinary how everybody took the water for granted.
Let there be water. Only vague suggestions
On origin of hydrosphere and atmosphere . . .

Not till Rubey, as late as 1951,
a paper still not in book form (1971), any serious contribution
To question how air and sea originated.
Take question of water first :
lakes, shallow seas forming many millions of years, not before
atmosphere,
But before atmosphere held any oxygen. Rubey rejects accepted
hypothesis

that the oceans condensed from primordial steam,
And postulates an entirely different source :
the degassing of the Earth's interior, by way of volcanoes,
hot springs, geysers,
Calculating that if you take the annual discharge of water
from hot springs in USA alone, plus half as much again
To cover submarine springs,
and multiply that figure by 3 billion years,
It gives you enough water produced from the Earth's interior
to fill all the lakes with their tranquillity,
or all the seas, their sorrow.

Rubey grants that some of the steam from hot springs
derives from surface water.
But if only 8% is juvenile, originated from Earth's mantle,
it could in geological time have filled entire volume of oceans.
Lyric of simplicity.
For water content of magmas, he gives 4% for basalts,
8% for deep granite;
Taking the lower figure, the 4%, calculates
that as igneous rocks contain 1% water
This would mean 3% was given off during crystallisation.
A shell of rock round the Earth only 40 kilometers thick
Would therefore account for all the water in all the world.
Lyric of simplicity.

As to my image of 'a blind Earth
turning within its envelope of darkness
Beneath a shroud: atmosphere of ammonia, methane and steam',
Rubey made me realise these lines were bad, inaccurate,
Because as he points out, if those gases had been the original atmosphere
the first rain would have been acid
And dissolved the ferrous bases of the rocks . . .
Towards Standards of Literary Criticism?

This hypothesis that squalling brat of sea
was taken out of Earth's own rib of rock,
Hands of night tugging teats of time,
milking a granite udder,
Till these reckless cavalry of waves
ride with their white manes flying, flying . . .
Can-can dancers with knickers of spray kicking and dancing
Or with limbs of surf on this beach lie dying, dying . . .
is as imaginative, more credible than Genesis,
And recently supported by mass spectrometer findings
of sea water taken from depth of 8,200 meters
Which show mantle also source
of excess Helium^{-3} and Helium^{-4}.

The first seas then : shallow seas.
    Not a molten earth cooling, more probably
A cool earth slowly heating up
    by gravitation, nuclear fission and possibly
Effect of lunar capture.
Cloud, junior in no sense,
    observing stromatolites at Steeprock, Lake Ontario
Signifying that tides were probably greater there 2-3 aeons ago,
    concluded Moon already in orbit then.
He had found similar evidence in Swaziland system.
And seeking some thermal event an aeon previous
    to explain the oldest known metamorphic and granite rocks,
And the lead isotope composition of various minerals
    indicating partial melting, and degassing of Earth's crust then,
Cloud suggests that this might have been caused
    by Moon's capture into Earth's orbit
3.4 – 3.6 aeons ago.

This hypothesis, supported by Moon's density and inclination of orbit,
    an event more than sufficient to explain
My image of tides of molten rock. Indeed, problem is :
    how capture didn't vaporise Earth, disintegrate Moon ?
Possibly, prograde rather than retrograde capture,
    how total catastrophe avoided ?
But this partial catastrophe would have melted Earth's crust
    sufficient to generate degassing,
Support Rubey's origin of hydrosphere and atmosphere
    from mantle, and even my own hot air,
Or was it 'clouds of steam' ?

Sufficient, too, to explain glass-like conduits on Moon's surface.
    But if Earth is 4.5 aeons old (and Baranov now suggested 7.5 !),
And Moon is 3.5,
    where did the Moon potter for this difference
While the blind Earth without eyes of seas
    turned and never found a shore ?

In the asteroid belt? Gradual accretion there,
  eventual capture by gravity?

An hypothesis (a series of holes tied together, a fishing net
  to trawl a shoal of stars).
But Cloud's desk calculation based on observation of stromatolites:
  Moon 3.5 old,
Confirmed by Apollo's scoop of lunar dust.
The moon: Earth's window to the world
Through which we can see Earth in its infancy,
On which we will hear planets birthing: and know
  nothing was, but is;
  nothing is, but will be . . .

The first seas then: shallow seas.
The seas had to emerge before life,
  or death evolved.
For a thousand million years, my hunch is more,
  an Earth without free oxygen,
A thin atmosphere of CO_2 and N,
  leaving one with a series of apparent paradoxes:
While oxygen itself is a derivative of life . . .
  Not very encouraging. Most confusing.
No wonder I failed to answer her last letter
  in time, her time. . . .

To precis the matter (poetry = crystallisation):
  oxygen generated by photosynthesis:
(What poet could write it simpler?)
  $CO_2 + H_2O + \text{light energy} \text{———} CH_2O + O_2$.
Or the equation and process can be reversed
  by the oxidation of carbohydrate molecule:
$CH_2O + O_2 \text{———} CO_2 + H_2 + \text{energy}$,
  to explain the dry cow grazing outside my window
Or this paw-like hand which holds this pen.
  Using the isotope O_{18} as a tracer,

Carbon dioxide is revealed as the source
Of the oxygen atoms of the synthesised organic molecules,
    and molecular oxygen acts as an acceptor for H_2 atoms,
As a sink : in all processes a sink.
    Is this case the sink is biological oxidation.
In fermentation yielding CO_2 and ethanol;
    in respiration, water. The energy
Liberated by such oxidation-reduction reactions
    makes for synthesis, energy batteries
Such as adenosine triphosphate (ATP),
    a biological trigger.

    The paradox how the cell which requires oxygen
protects itself from toxic effect of free oxygen,
    resolved by existence of organless, peroxisomes,
Enzymes which reduce free oxygen molecules
    to amino acids. Metabolism, not a mystery.
Multicellular organisms evolving haemoglobin
    to store surplus oxygen to release into blood
After exertion. Whose blood
    streams in the firmament ?

Not, then, oxygen giving birth to life, but life itself
    the source of oxygen. None of this gas,
Or practically none, could have emerged from Earth's interior,
    from vulcanism and Rubey's outgassing,
Nor it is included in igneous rock;
    therefore – what diamond is this word,
Through what tangles, through what jungles have we swung
    to grasp it ? And what have we but reason ? –
Therefore, the first organisms must have been anaerobes
    depending on fermentation; and an heterotroph,
Procaryotic cell, incapable of photosynthesis, of manufacturing own
    food, evolved about 3 billion years ago into an autotroph,
Organism capable of feeding : creatures, then,
    eucaryotic, which left their signature on rock
Which Cloud deciphers.

He identifies the banded iron formation in Minnesota
  as oxidised marine sediments laid down in open bodies of water.
Since iron there is ferric (Fe^{+++}), not reduced ferrous (Fe^{++}),
  it indicates that there was at least 1.8 billion years ago
A source of oxygen in the column of water,
  suggesting that the first oxygen-releasing photoautotrophs
May have used ferrous compounds in solution
  as oxygen acceptors,
Oxygen for them being a waste product: a sink.
  Always a sink. (Perhaps that is what matter is –
Litter left by light on the lawns of space? . . .)
  This would have precipitated iron in ferric form:
$4\,FeO + O_2 \longrightarrow 2\,Fe_2O_3$.
  'And once oxygen mediating enzymes arose,
Oxygen generated by increasing population of photoautotrophs
  containing these enzymes would build up in the ocean
And escape into the atmosphere.' A sink.

  Then, not merely possibly
But probably, UV-irradiation from sun
  would dissociate some of the molecular oxygen
Into highly reactive atomic oxygen and ozone.
  Both, with O_2, leading to oxidisation of iron in surface rocks,
Making for the redbeds such as in Grand Canyon,
  the second producing the ozone screen in uper atmosphere
A protective blanket filtering out toxic rays.

  Another possible source of oxygen in photolysis,
The dissociation of water vapour in the outer atmosphere,
  followed by the escape of the H_2 from gravitational field.
But this source probably small. No figure obtainable here.
  The whole tapestry of the oxygen cycle
Essentially vague, but no longer mysterious. No need for a metaphor
  to describe the process: the miracle is squared
By being partially understood:
  organised eucaryotic cell metabolism

At least 1.3 billion years old;
    life breeding life,
Life yielding oxygen which built to ozone screen
    to trigger photosynthesis on sea surface
Accelerating build-up further,
    making metazoan organisms possible, say 640 million years ago,
As O_2 replaced CO_2 in the atmosphere. . . .
    We can breathe, because chalk settles.

Earth, sea, air : one element, interdependent,
    an ecological unit, to preserve
Or to pollute, make up your mind
    while you've still got a mind.
A cycle so intricate that to quote a geologist, not a poet :
    'the next breath you breathe will contain
Atoms exhaled by Jesus at Gethsemane
    and Hitler at Munich'. Not may,
But will. A metaphor I knew
    but did not dare. Geology is poetry
Where poetry is true.

CANTO TWENTY-ONE

SILURIAN

Marine: entirely marine,
  but unlike Ordovician
Free from vulcanicity; a shallow fresh-water sea,
  covering most of Wales, the Southern Uplands,
A large slice of the Lake District; the sea silting
  mud and debris falling through the water; the Bala series:
Sandstones, conglomerate bands, greywrackes, maroon green shales,
  and coarse detritus, in places 10,000
Diminishing to 300 feet thick, indicating
  sea floor under pressure: slipping
Or creeping, tilting and folding,
  faulting, slumping then contorting,
Grooving and slickensiding, here and there
  a shoulder shoved out of the sea,
Wave motion eroding
  causing further silting,
Revealed by overlaps and overlays.

A mine of fossils:
  dolomites, with prominent compound eyes,
The usual brachipods, grapholites,
  but fewer corals, too much mud;
And crinoids ousting cystideans.
  Then, in Lower Ludlow: a seam of ancestors,
I can begin to write I:
  the first vertebrates appear.

Lampreys, hagfish and shark,
  skeletons of savagery:
Scorpions forty feet long,
  grubbers in the mud,
Feeders on flatfish.
  The lampreys, boneless, jawless,

Limbless and mouthless, with their sucking disc and single eye :
    wholly parasitical, fastening on other fish,
Sucking their entrails, wholly parasitical,
    but in spite of those habits,
Not quite relatives. . . .
    Yet these spineless lampreys and the ostracoderms,
Slunking on the sea bottom with their shell-encased skin
    as some protection from the scorpions,
Probably the species from which vertebrates evolved,
    when the shallow fresh-water seas
Were swamped by salt water
    causing them to stir off their bellies in the mud
Where silt and debris had fed them.
    They searched for food in the deep clear water,
Preyed on other fish, needed a jaw,
    and in blind hunger bit their way to teeth,
In shoaled terror swam their way to fins,
    finding in mobility, the shark's ferocity.
Once predatory, we can say we;
    Those seas deep in screams, the tides
Entire terror :
    to bite, to begin; to prey,
To progress; our kind, not from kindness.
    By fit, we mean the crude was cruel,
By fittest, the most cruel.
    It is all in the pain,
Either receptacles or instruments of pain;
    a conjugation of cruelty;
All in the pain.

NOTES

The Rape of Lucretia. The libretto for Benjamin Britten's opera was first published by Boosey & Hawkes in 1945, and the work was first performed at Glyndebourne in the following year. The Interlude describes Tarquinius's ride to Rome. The strong rhythm of the verse combined with that of the music gives a vivid impression of irresistible forward motion. The Lullaby is sung by the Female Chorus over Lucretia's sleeping form just prior to the rape. Originally the opera ended with the passacaglia ensemble of mourning over Lucretia's body with the words 'Is this it all? It is all'. At the suggestion of the composer, the librettist added the Epilogue in Canzone form to complete the framework of the pagan tragedy as seen through Christian eyes. There is a complete recording of *The Rape of Lucretia* on Decca SET 492–3.

This Way to the Tomb (Faber & Faber, 1946). This verse drama was first performed at the Mercury Theatre in 1945, produced by E. Martin Browne and with music by Britten. It later transferred to the Garrick Theatre, running in all for some 18 months. In the classical form of masque and anti-masque, it recounts the temptations of St Antony, who determines to fast unto death on the island of Zante and renounces all known sins only to have that of spiritual pride revealed in all its nakedness. The play is shot through with Canzoni, of which this is the last.

The Eagle has two Heads (Vision Press, 1946). This free adaptation of Cocteau's *La Mort écoute aux portes* was first performed at the Haymarket Theatre in 1946, and subsequently transferred to the Globe. The roles of the Queen and her would-be assassin were played by Eileen Heirlie and James Donald. Cocteau later changed the French title to *L'Aigle à deux têtes*, thereby waspishly implying a mistranslation of a title that never was. The extract here is from Act III.

'Hylas', 'Canzone', 'Aubade', 'Briony', 'Song', 'The Mason's Epitaph' and 'Practical Ballad' were all first published in *The Mongrel and other poems* (Faber & Faber, 1950). The cantata 'Hylas', again in strict canzone form, was written for Kathleen Ferrier after her astounding success in *Lucretia*, was not set by Britten as was originally intended, but was later by Stanley Glasser. The birth celebrated in 'Canzone' is that of the writer's daughter Briony, who is also the subject of the poem of that name. 'Aubade' and 'Song' experiment with form as indicated. Both 'The Mason's Epitaph' and 'Practical Ballad', the former a tribute to a Devon craftsman, are token of the poet's constant concern with practical matters.

Stratton (Faber & Faber, 1950). A psychological verse drama, with music by Britten, centred upon a man who murders his son – a reversal of ancient fertility myths. It was first performed in Brighton in 1949 with Clive Brook in the lead. The play was considerably rewritten during rehearsal, and fearsome production difficulties during the pre-West End tour caused the author to withdraw it. He has since radically recast the play under the new title *From Father to Son*. The extract here is Stratton's soliloquy in Act III, and the other character referred to is his wife, stricken with hysterical blindness. The published postscript was not to be played.

The Death of Satan (Faber & Faber, 1955). First performed at the Devon Festival in 1954, and later at the Royal Court, the play is an extended conversation in hell between Oscar Wilde, George Bernard Shaw and Lord Byron. In this excerpt Satan, condemned to death since God, too, is dead, curses the world.

'The Solitudes' and 'Air Raid' were first published in *The Solitudes* (Faber & Faber, 1961). The love poems 'The Solitudes' were written for Virginia Maskell. No. 19 opens with an image taken from an earlier poem which was incorporated into Act I of *Lucretia* at Britten's suggestion and finds its final form here; the poem is a single Canzone strophe. No. 20 is also in strict form, and this poem was particularly admired by T. S. Eliot. The image of the severed hand in 'Air Raid' was also used as the motto for the oratorio *Mea Culpa*, written for Britten after Hiroshima, which, for complicated reasons involving publishers and the BBC, was never set. The poem itself commemorates a wartime raid on Brixton, where the writer lived before World War II.

'Heloise to Abelard' is the seventh letter (of twelve) in *Abelard and Heloise*, a 'Correspondence for the Stage' first performed at the Arts Theatre in 1960 and published by Faber & Faber in the following year. The play was written for Virginia Maskell and closely based on the surviving letters between the historical lovers.

'Easter Lullaby', 'Ascension', 'The Gift' and 'For a Dying Woman' are from *Unpopular Poems* (Rupert Hart-Davis, 1969). 'Ascension' suggests that if Christ had foreseen the misery and violence caused by the religious organization that took his name, he might have worked out the passion within himself rather than externalized it. 'The Gift' is for the poet's wife, and 'The Dying Woman' for her mother.

Man. Parts I and II were published by The Rebel Press in 1970 and 1971 respectively. The whole poem comprises five parts which has now been published in its entirety by the Rebel Press (distributed by The Compton Press Ltd). Part I examines the concepts of time, space and energy within the context of human consciousness, and the Canto 'Eraze' is one of many which chronicle the emergence of the planet earth. Part II deals with the origins of matter. The long Canto 'Archean' is a fair example of the method used throughout the poem, the rejection of 'poetic' usage in favour of the didactic, almost Socratic framework of discovery. The last sentence of this Canto could almost be described as the germ of the whole work. In 'Silurian' the first stirrings of life on earth are vividly imagined.